United States distributor

DUFOUR EDITIONS, INC.

Booksellers and Publishers

Chester Springs, Pennsylvania 19425

BRASS RUBBINGS

BRASS RUBBINGS

David Day

A CARCANET PRESS PUBLICATION

For Cynthia

Notes concerning individual poems in the "Brass Rubbing" sequence: ii. The nicety of a completed rubbing seems very much to depend on an initial stage, discovering the shapes by pressure made on the paper, before any shading is started. v. Brass rubbers, generally, would not think grey images successful. vii. Facsimiles are increasingly being offered as substitutes for worn brasses. xv. Brass rubbers would want to class this discovery as a palimpsest. xxi. It is often felt that a rubbing is a failure if missing parts of the brass have not been denoted. xxv. M. B. S. — the Monumental Brass Society. xxvii. It is easy to spoil a rubbing by allowing the wax to mark the paper beyond the edge of the figure.

Although the "Brass Rubbing" poems appear in the order in which they were written, owing to the need to make exclusions, the sequence lacks its original numbering.

SBN 85635 121 0

Acknowledgements are due to *Phoenix, P. E. N. New Poems 1971-72*, the Southern Arts Association, *Delta, Workshop, The New York Times*, the Cellar Press, *Poetry Nation, Critical Quarterly, Poetry Now* (B. B. C.), *Encounter*, and the *Times Literary Supplement*.

First published 1975 by
Carcanet Press Limited
266 Councillor Lane
Cheadle Hulme, Cheadle
Cheshire SK8 5PN

Printed in Great Britain
by W & J Mackay Limited, Chatham
by photo-litho

CONTENTS

BRASS RUBBINGS

THE MILL

It was rare the sense of wheel
and water left us: most rooms
had a suggestion of the movement.
We used to put our ears against
the biggest timbers.
Thin fibre never had much resonance.

The race foamed on into the dark
cleft, ripped through ages
into rock between our house and mill
(boys like us had fished for its depth).

Since the Conqueror our mill had straddled
the town's river that cut through
fields and gardens to slip narrowed
rushing in our channel.
There was argument
about our ancient water-rights.

Getting in the way
meant that an uncle used to flail us
with his dusty cap. Clouds
came from our heads. My grandfather would smile
and lead us to his "port-hole"
where he used to let us look
a foot above the thunder of the water-wheel.

Its ceaseless turgid revolution held us. Green
greasy steps led to its creaking side.
Water tumbled, scooped and tossed.
Hands of pale reflected light circled
as they slithered from the stair.
Sun-atoms spilled
in the water's arc and darkened down
they made a sediment. We used to dredge
for it in jars, then mount the steps,
watching how the cloud would fine
into a glassiness. We never thought
that one small slip might stain the water.

Sometimes, a "water-wheeling god" would open up
the trap and with a white inverted head
shout rough warnings. Jawing actions
in the din were feigned replies.

So much for deus-ex-machina. Mouthing
didn't matter much to us.

There were those who thought the sunless side
a safe place by the mill-pool, mould
of the stream's downward sweep, dark bowl
mooned by casual eddies. This was sullen water
absent from the wheel's crash.
Shadow-fish suggested presences
but rarely rose to peering callow boys.
Opaque and dumb.
We whipped the face with willow sticks
but only made a dash of froth.
Hectic, we wanted something more
and thrashed it till we tired.

       Evenings
meant the bigger wheels were taken off
(One small mill worked by a diversion.
The river's level always had to reach
the highest mark).
There was chatter in the house.
Girls at mirrors witnessed a vibration:
slightly rippling images became them.
Then they fancied streaming hair
and perhaps progressive poses. A big conceit.

Down stream round the stepping-stones
the water whispered
into our green deep special pool.
We used to watch an age
to see the very heavy fish move. They kept
the pressure which sustained their stillness
in the current.

IN PREP

The tabulations are relieved by pictures.
We conjugate some words. The magister
disturbs the heavy air as he slips
by. His gown is full

a moment, then he takes his place
where he observes our cubicles. He sniffs,
at which I make a phrase so firmly, roundly
it must groove the page. A chance air shifts

an illustration of a nymph
as a blackbird starts a kind of song.
Things in the garden are as they should be;
the lawn shows shadow from the giant buttress;

the sun has gone behind the tower.
Sometimes a creaking chair implies the restlessness,
determination of a boy as he describes
a word, a shape of which he is uncertain.

The scent of stock comes through the window.

ON "MEETING" DR LEAVIS AND HIS WIFE
*   IN A NORTHERN SECOND-HAND BOOKSHOP*

Squatting and roofed by a wedge of dusty sunlight
from the skylight above,
I, obscure in my nether world,
inhaled the rank
of Shakespeare "Scholars' Texts".
Tall the two seemed now again,
yet, cut off at waist together in the drifting light,
strangely odd,
flown north from Luddites
bruising Brooke's countryside.
A far cry this from King's Parade
and high matters of discrimination.

Was there to be no more
harpooning
books on spiky phrases?
And then:
"Surely dear, one has all
    the Ruskin one wants!"
The bald pate gleamed,
and nodding down
one quick sharp glance
saw Scholars' Texts,
and pulped them with a sigh.

VIRGINIA WOOLF

I unpin my hat. I know that
is not in words. The dragonfly which shifts
suspends its gleam by no means,
in its wings. Seeing the unseen
is touching water, rings
that memorize a swallow's wing.
The herbage is alive
with too much sense of intertwining
business that cannot speak.
It flows as shadows pass; paths
are filled I found to come here.

I unpin my hat no matter
if you find it as the rest is
names of water flowers that I add
as I approach the verge of yielding
consciousness. It is sinking
in a sheath of green and cold
dispersing light to bursting
lungs and silent blackness as it comes.

HELEN AND EDWARD THOMAS SAY GOODBYE
TO EACH OTHER FOR THE LAST TIME

Calling through a wood:
each voice grew faint, she going
to their child and he towards
the train. How did they divide?

She did not ask him why
he fought and he explained by crumbling soil.

He wrote as if
he never could return. Some images,
old nests, a cripple, sowing in sweet dust
expressed the age he had encompassed,
classic looks impaired.

                Each must have stopped
to wonder if the other called again.

JOHN CLARE MEETS HIS PATRON

In the sun among his rich possessions
he looks small and settled.
His dark coat supports his slender frame.
He must be a proper man.

I do not approach
until they say. My thoughts go back
to the broken bird which lay
by our step. The food we offered

made it screech with angry pain.
Its open throat looked raw.
When it was gone
there was a gentle shape made by its breast

behind the flowers. I found her
by her golden eye
among the green. Then someone softly touches
me and says it is the lord

who waves me down. He speaks
in a kindly way and I make phrases,
though we do not talk. He smiles.
It is gracious to be bidden

here and told to go
John Clare and come again to read.
The noonday sun is spread
through his estate. "There was this hurt

creature . . .": suddenly and out of turn.
"Write more!" he said and looked away.
As I tread home along hot dusty roads
and paths I make as if to imitate

an order that he gave. One gesture
in the air and it was done. No one can see
my hand describe the arc.
I need the shade as much as he.

JOHN CLARE AND THE SNAKES

It was hard to tell who people were
as I came home. The shapes of faces
hung in dusky doors. The lamp by me
gutters, though it glares as if

the bowl is full. Each day we work
in unrelenting heat. We cannot rest.
Behind the drape the family toss
and turn, the woman fetching

breath like the death-rattle.
She told me had I seen the adders
round the pail as I came in;
their filth is from their breeding

in the dung; the milk is ruined
once again; your mother shouted through
the men were forced to hold you
in the threshing yard; you had killed

the snake that you would not stop hitting.
It is true that I became aware
there was a viper twisting, sticking
on my flail. They set my back

against the grain and said, "Stay there".
But I must make my brain conform
to steps, and walking in the dark
could be a way, though on the heath the fires

are never still. And then I want to say
things in a fashion that I cannot understand.
A creature that I met as Frenchmen
being led in chains went by

declared that they would always take
his wares. He smashed a serpent's head
and strung its length with others bleeding
on his pole, then held them high to shade

his leering face: "Is that John Clare?" he said.

JOHN CLARE, DISMISSED

A moon is at the edge
of cloud, a night storm gathering
when we have finished
our day's work. They let me have the wain

until I leave it empty
in the field where I lie down.
One end makes bars
across the heavy reddened face.

They say they will not have me
working here again. "Moon-calf!"
one roared and flung away
my fork. Which keeps on touching

far away, small prongs without
a distant grumbling, the hurt
the darkness will sustain
upon its rim. Beggars' bowls I can act out

with hands, but fens are endless.
It was because I could not trim
the load which fell. Imagining
is all my fault. I felt the wheat

should not ride true, the balance be
in emptiness. "Let the sun
glare through!": as they all cursed.
There was a child who stared at me.

JOHN CLARE IN THE BITTER COLD SPRING

The mad must be outside
now it is Spring. The sun is driven
by the clouds across our field.
The men and women can make little

of the rows because the strips of light
are moving fast. One points his implement
towards the sky. The attendants tell him
it is far too cold to stop. The North Wind

covers wastes and seas before
it reaches us. Here, the blackthorn
loads the wood with snow. The contours
open, fold and taunt

my flesh. Breeding images
need not be satisfying though. They cannot
make the man bring down his hoe. A wild
snatch comes over: "Let him grow,

a frozen thing". The strange folk chatter
round him, then one runs and several moan
and try to huddle up like people.
They are enfeebled. Last year,

their faces quickly darkened in the blast.
They were nearly motionless:
they nudged the earth and made a foot
or two of progress in the weed.

JOHN CLARE, WITH HIS RELATIONS AGAIN

In apple-trees the fruit
is swaying in the flowing field.
All the movement comes at me.
Bad perspectives shift my brain.

There is whispering
that they are testing me again.
There must be rivers in the grain.
I know that Northborough

means Mary in her pale blue gown.
When I was stumbling on from day
to dark I entertained the body
as a sheath of white. Gainsaying spirit,

hunger, pain as one is lies. The absence
of our touching is insane.
Her grave shows signs
she died long since.

But grass can taste like bread
and I can walk the miles,
protest that I am there
for all my strength, strike light

from nakedness like Tom O' Bedlam,
ordinary flesh. My hand,
a chalky pebble clenched,
looks meaningless upon the moss, a bed.

Nameless roundness is no more
than I can need, a woman says
and glides away. And at my garden's end
she joins a set. They turn

to hear me shake away
a senseless pun about landscape.
I try to concentrate about the fact
the earth was often calm when I worked

in the fields a hundred miles away.

JOHN CLARE, CONSTRAINED

Rime is my coat.
I have slept out all night.
Trees are happy in December dazzle.
That I live is no concern of theirs.

The sun is over Burghley House.
The master wakes and calls
through gilded corridors. I walked
from Newark to be here.

Work is here. I felt mad to be
constricted so by tents and bugles' call.
Some told me of the river's bore.
The bowing Trent was mine as well.

Birds ran through my brain
and mice which nibbled
in the straw. Crows cawed
and settle in the wicked elms.

In sleep my nodding head was loath
to know if women wait.
Outside, I can unbend
my book and roam with

letters in a ploughman's hand.
I make my furrow, hoe my field,
have set my seed.
Those women know that

I am mad. They look askance,
make mouths they think
I cannot read. Dumb creatures
realize a stare.

I know how creatures care:
a nervous vole, a creeping mole,
a pasty new-born rat which writhes,
a maggot in a dead man's hole.

Birds scream in millions,
blacken fields and tear the grass
for food. But I could show
them insects where the humans

grow. Tonight, will that man
want this fragment from
my hand? I am arrested
here. I discourse in a lair.

CLARE, FINALLY

I do not know why I am
here. The letters are like birds
that rise disturbed and wheel
across my page, a little sky.

I rub the edges, feel my way
by syllables, those tender shoots
that curl and wither underneath
my tears. The paper is a pitted scene.

I try to shuffle blackened seeds,
but they perform a frenzied game.
I gaze: a master picks
out words which twist like tails.

This Literature has spoiled my head,
no faces, figures, speech
to tell the separation of my dreams.
There are only eddies in the stream.

"THIS IS A SCENE FOR SUNSHADES"

This is a scene for sunshades,
the people lounging on the lawn
behind a country house. The enclosing
garden wall supports ripening pears.

There are few remarks because
the heat-wave is prolonged.
The master of the house, a widower, is sitting
where a draught can reach him

in his chair. His white hair just shows
inside the darkened room. Back to back,
the lovers share a rug, pretending
they are not yet properly acquainted. She sips

her lemon-tea and flicks the pages
of a magazine. The man winds up his time-piece
as he pauses over a review which he is writing.
A married pair drift off because they hear

a distant sound, a bell, a call.
The centres are where touches cannot pall.
The girl remembers how last night he was
a silhouette against the moonless dark.

Their flesh was something else, apart.
The cold clear star suspended
from Orion's belt pulsed once
beside her lover's head, and then he moved.

"HAVING BEEN TO TASTE A NEIGHBOUR'S
    FLOWER WINE"

Having been to taste a neighbour's flower wine
and climbing a broad path
against the wind, I reach the brow
and face the stars. Keen frost has crisped

the grass. There are no intervening hills
or villages. The only light is from the sky.
I breathe hard, which adds to the bouquet. Just
off the tip of a great jointed constellation

like a tentacle there's the faintest finger-
print. And there are other minute clusters
which are hardly there. It would be good
to feel the air, I'd said and left them

by the fire. They'd raised their glasses
to me. And now I tilt my head and link
two gleaming planets. "The wine!"
I say aloud into the dark.

AN OLD LADY IN HER GARDEN

She can move the earth though very old.
Underneath a waterfall of blossom
she turns the surface of her garden.
Her frailty must have the depth
of freshness in the shade.

TESTING ICE

Boys cry, "Will it bear?":
we wait on the edge of ice.
It is past New Year.
My uncle tests the strength

and grins. The wind cuts
in. I turn away a youthful face
again from that black hole
which gapes where he whose name

I never knew was drowned. Uncle!
I still see you there
and can't associate your boldness
with the hands which try to grip,

a body for a moment held
by water and one desperate stare
towards the sky for friends:
you stand and see us slide

as we shout back it groans, it bends.
In the bitter air I see your mill-coat
dragged against your frame. You wave
and leave us to the game,

but you return to scan across
the palings, making sure we go
when lights come on. Then I think
you might well try it on your own again.

ON THE WAY HOME

A short stretch of rubble went to
their back yards. Nothing could grow there.
That was where the simple ageing man lived
with the other people in a row. After rain,
they'd unsneck their doors and blink into the watery sun,
wave absently to me, smile for no special reason.
From an old factory there was a steady under-burr.

One Saturday he crossed briefly to my stop,
and, picking up my cricket pads, he pretended
he might put them on. When he straightened:
"Tha' was rained off then. Yet it wasn't such a storm."
"Big enough for us, I fear."
"Well, I were lying down." Storms
he'd seen I guessed: the pre-war strikes,
friends mangled in the pit, blood
in the pub spitoon . . . and then
there was his present state,
the haunted carcinoma-look, sallow and distrait,
and, having said what he could say,
the shallow breathing as he shuffled off.

The dust showed slurs, unlike the way he spoke.

PAINTERS IN THE MINSTER

In their whites, the workmen mount
their ladders. Dean and Chapter criticize
the conduct of the task. The men go carefully,
hand over hand. The space is vast.

All the people going round
create a baffled undertow of sound.

The painters, having risen to the roof,
need not experience a special awe.
It is probable that they have seen a fall.
They feel their climb:
they huff a little
dust before they start a staring cornice
or a girlish king. They work with blobs
and touches, face the stone again,
put colours in some obscure places.
These firm journeymen make progress.

Knowing where he is, one stops to watch
his fellow brush a head which grows
from his: they share a corner in the air.

THREE GARGOYLES

Puckered in a common sneer
almost top side this squat church-
tower, a blackened chunk against
the teasing fleece of clouds.
Their nostrils are flared at such pie.
One stump for each to chomp
a thickened upper lip, they spew
arcs which drill graves,
perhaps tickle a rib or two.
Their comic mason took his chance.
He envisaged a gurgling fall,
could spot the mark that he would hit,
relieved his feelings from on high.

THE COUPLE

For a time the news
of this discovery spoiled
this grips. We part the fronds
again. The two long people form

a whole; their lips pushed out
to kiss stem from
their non-existent brows, and then
their shoulders have one arm;

the phallus in her loins
is out the other side; there
even is a line to link
their knees; he takes the weight,

his feet astride; her legs are roundly
joined. The couple had to seem
completely bound. The sun
is blinding on the rock. Then having

let the fern spring back,
we crouch beneath to eat
our food. Deep summer here. No words
of mine could intimate

the drowsy intermittent bird-song's exact
quality. The stream, just near, pushing
higher, leaves a line. We munch away.
I do not disturb her thoughts

as we keep still and sun ourselves,
then at a rumble underground
she smiles and whispers, "Cave-men!"
"Quarrying," I say and think

no one could tell, if they could see,
that we were married, sitting here.

A BELL ON THE GROUND

The lip is tilted in the soil and catches
the sea wind, though there are many acres
from the ruin to the last hedge
where the land cannot be sown.

The bell is overgrown by willow-herb
in flower. We can see the fire's black
stain where it was sucked
into the upper tower. The flash bursting through

the roof was like a momentary crown across the fen,
although close watchers never heard the bell fall
— it was hung so centrally it did not touch the stone.
The light and the long heavy notes were strong

that night. The gale was high. We comment on
their need to have the tower
so far inland to get their bearing
in the dark. "Let them look up", says the scroll

beneath the waving green. Along this slope
the grass is lush and flowers are various
and plentiful. We say we understand
why men at sea would want both light and sound.

AT "THE PILGRIMS' WAY"

We are ranged along a dusty gallery
and someone claims, among the babble,
that the bell below his feet responds to sound.
His lips moving and his sing-song accent register

remotely as I think that down the coast,
when floods came in the night, the people clinging
to their roofs heard distant bells fired
time and time again. Reaching out below us

is the river mouth which pilgrims used to cross
despite the risk. Balancing in
creeping out, then getting down, to find
the tenor's name is "Omega", there is the problem

of the process in the frieze around the lip.
Others follow. We often mindlessly read out
the martyr's name. Among the runes
there is a linking face with narrow eyes,

whilst swastikas denote the bell's power. Then
at the different vents we try to see an indication
of the point at which we started early on
this morning. Half way to the island and its church

we observed that, when high winds got in
behind the tide, the final fleet would have to take
a sudden torrent. And we know now
that pilgrims had to kneel at certain points

to say set prayers. On display are rosaries
recovered from the drowned. Nor is the possibility
of rescue mentioned. The wind begins to rise and sough
inside the tower. Then as we leave, descend,

the thought of Braille and telling beads occurs
to me: on the string I handled there were letters
which the stranded person could have tried to feel,
although to hold himself against the gale

he would have had to tense himself
and bend repeatedly. As we go down, we turn
and turn again. The spiral seems to tighten
in the dark. It must have been that as the sea rushed

in, his lips were moving rapidly according to a prayer.

BRASS RUBBINGS (i)

The paper is arranged
to rub a brass. I kneel.
The action of the church's
clock taps softly in
the tower. I am lulled by movement
on the figure that appears:
streaks become an even shade
with steady lines. No hand shakes
as I make out a satisfying piece.
I rest upon a composition.

Nothing disturbs this attitude.
Straight walking with my picture
rolled, I pass through graves,
down steps and under walls
accumulating heat.
So firmly brass absorbs
a feeling disposition.

(ii)

To keep the paper tight I seal
him in. This place seems airless.
The image is not proud. Now
and then a gleam comes through

the cloud, but he has no window
near. It is difficult to feel the line
and several times, with crayon poised,
I've wavered by the head:

in knowing that this brass is fine
I cannot chance my arm.
Then lying down to see
what angles can reveal, I think

there is the faintest smile,
at which I stand to paddle him
in stockinged feet, a tip from
an enthusiast that seemed absurd.

Yet there he is in hollows,
not a mark to spoil the curls,
the delicate complexity of mail,
the stars, the stance among the flowers.

(iii)

Rising air disturbs the drapes.
Blinds tap as the sun bears down.
At home, we want to free our clothes,
but there are open doors. Ascending

stairs, I pass another girl, this
one coming from a white surround
and caught by an inscription
at her waist. With nothing more below

this dark maiden sways; her tresses
float, her bodice undulates
and turns. I stop her movement,
touching where the heart would be.

36

(iv)

Replacing the carpet over her, over
him, I feel where I am again.
The sparrows are eating the crumbs
of my lunch in the porch. I can see

where a mason has chipped out
his sign as an axe. The light enters
a chink in the door. The need
to be working again has gone through.

Subsiding, I glance at the debris,
the masking-tape, weights, scissors
and paper. The case of gold crayon
is closed. The feel of it ends

at my tips, demarcations,
the qualified grasp
in the actions that last
in the figure, the person.

It is the time that it takes me
gives me the chance now, in resting,
to know the residual movement,
the strength of the heart.

(v)

A couple steadily come through.
Though on my own, I can't resist
a smile, for they will go in any hall.
Now in this tiny church,

where bareness and the cold prevail,
the rubbing can keep up
a little glow, although my circulation
generally is low. I think my hand

is close to how at last two hold
each other dear, for their affection
is a modest showing in the touch
of half-closed palms. A bachelor

might have the fingers so, but
something in my bones, though stiff
and fairly old, I hope can move
beyond the set repose.

Adjusting, going on and making sure
the couple do not move, confirms that
they are turning slightly. The colour
is precisely done with simple pressure.

The grey forms in a corner though.
It is a trick the wits perform
obliquely as I look away, towards
the outside of the paper.

I am inclined to smile again.
A greater warmth would mean
a firmer friction, black shapes
confined and good for any wall.

(vi)

It was late. The church was locked
again. As I had tramped across the countryside
I'd kicked through crusted snow.
I was planning rubbings

for the Spring. The spray had gone before me
all the way, but now
a skein of geese, just glimpsed
through elms, went out to sea

against a sentimental pinkish sky.
It seemed in this cold spell
each trek there had to be abortive.
And then the vicar breathily came up.

He had forgotten something. "Brasses?
  Yes, I have some. Do I know you?
  It might sound abrupt, but
  it's my duty to preserve what preciousness

  we have here. These once
  were argent, purple, ruby, all those rich shades
  which could proclaim nobility."
There was no colour left.

"Trampled off, of course!" he nearly shouted.
I thought about the windy light
of March, the broken watery dappling
on the sharp black cover I could give them.

Then as I stood in darkness by the floodlit crib
I noted that the man was ashen.

(vii)

The incumbent says he'll let me try a copy
of a brass. Its lines are blatant, far too sharp.
"Can't do much damage there, old chap!
    A pound! Cheap at the price!

    Yes, bluff remarks, but I can tell
    that you're no practised rubber, with your stumps of black
    and bits of paper." He waves my note and goes
whilst his sepulchral sounds are echoing and getting lost.

The decoration is excessive. Marble dandies
stand in Saxon àrches. The bishop on the brass
I'm not allowed to rub holds up two fingers; so
I think it worth the risk

to take a quick memento of this gesture.
Then down the lane and by the ford I look over
the worn hand that has a light stud
on the wrist. That touch reminds me

of the pleasant thinness, that the marks
had nearly gone, the metal seeming just a patina
not long before its disappearance. Then in this shaded place
beside the swiftly running water

it takes my fancy to snip round
the rubbing and to launch it.

(viii)

It is odd we cannot quite remember
when we took the rubbing
of a staring lord armed cap-a-pie.
It could have been last summer

in a chapel tucked among the Wolds.
Certainly the day was hazy. Sheep
were grazing through the graves.
His long frame took up the afternoon,

but, being lazy, taking turns, we none
of us appraised his size. Only
for a moment was his image raised
head high, for we had finished him

then cut him from the roll. I blew
through him that it was time
for tea and going home. But now
we see him constantly through open stairs,

and I suppose that it is simply where
he is that airs do not disturb him
when some lighter rubs a shade removed
have sometimes stirred. And now my daughters

sing and hurry past as they ascend
when it is dusk. I frequently approach,
yet cannot fix on any detail but the mass
and spaces in the face, intensifying

always as the darkness grows.

(ix)

She is very secret here.
Her grandfather is underneath the steps
not far away. Her bunches fly.
As the slight depression

in the ground denotes, her plinth has gone,
then as an amber curtain sways
a tinge of sun illuminates
this child's expression. But

the light grows dull to leave
the tarnished figure flush in stone.
The material gets in the way
and so I push it off, at which

the rings disturb a roosting bird.
In settling, its plaintiveness takes up
the sound the runners made. I only need
a small white page to bring her through

in azure with the lines as delicate
as finches' bones, the long straight dress
a fraction flared, bare feet
on tip-toe in the air.

42

(x)

In here, we can unwind. It is quiet
after driving through so many
unfamiliar urban places. A dove provides
the only sound from where saints

are a modest fire in evening sun.
It is strange to find a creamy robe
left casually across
a vestry chair. All these stray parts

before we rub a couple make
us pause. I let the colours rattle
in the box and think about
another pair who each hold out

a heart, simple when compared
with these who seem too fussy
in heraldic leaves, hands somewhere
twined, too many grooves because

they knew the Church was getting
secular. We know we're not far
away from the vaunted brass cadaver,
although, dogged, having lost some

of the early indecision in the silence,
we press on, achieve the rubbings
whilst there is sufficient light.
Her summer dress looks luminous as I assemble

our possessions in the dusk. She calls softly
down the church: "I have the rest of our belongings."

(xi)

It was not a day for rapid movement.
In a garden where the heat was banked
against deep trees, dehiscing broom
picked out how still it was. A fan-tail lifted

in the thermals by the tower.
The church's stone was very bright. High
in adjacent ash some leaves were wilting.
It occurred to me in quick succession

that the sap was now reduced, since
the wax might well have lost its firmness the result
might not be clear, that a status quo
can be too enervating, visualizing how

the rubbing hand goes
up and down, advancing. Inside the church,
our brass, epitomizing much that once
was rich, was lying in a private place.

Beneath a window where the stained striations
helped to moderate the sun an old woolman
with a wry expression looked at ease
as I brought out his heavy ermined shape

again, until, where I'd forgotten
what was at the base, there was no date,
no moral, name, which gave
the cool black rub clean isolation.

44

(xii)

It must be since the war
that they took down a martyr's brass
and gave him pride of place, it seems,
as I examine him among some flags

they gather on the fen. Outside, low down,
you can make out the holes
which give a kneeling shape. It was a brass
to represent a lady who endowed the tower.

The martyr, placed above the clock to look across
the marsh, was certainly the subject of the local cult
which she had instituted. Flower arrangements,
plush and order seem incongruous

as I associate this area with war-
time service, though the only dead we saw
were parts of an old fowler who had lost
his way. It was largely waiting, cold

and mist, some tramping up and down
a virtually flat piece they called a causeway. Then
there were the absurd challenges we had to make
when it was dark. "A bloody riot!"

someone said not long before we heard
the mine go off. I often think about the figure
in the wind; his head tilts sadly
as he bends to grip his staff.

(xiii)

Refusing to believe it could be cold
I get up early, take my box
and, lightly clad, set out across
the fields. The grass is drenched

in dew and it is white like frost,
a robin cheeps, the sun is weak
and the sky is only pallid.
I cross the last stile which was lost

beneath the darkness of a yew
and hurry through the churchyard to
the door, at which I fleetingly take in
the scratch-dial which is visible because

the sun is low. The brass I go
to rub could be the meagre bellman who
could only say his offices. His head is slightly
to one side, one cheek is hollow; brasses often

are just formal, though he looks pathetic
pressing palms together, all his decoration
being one or two bent crosses. The cold
in here makes its impression,

and so, stepping over, near the figure, scraps
discarded yesterday because of unsuccessful efforts,
I decide it might be warmer rubbing in
a patch of dusty sunlight.

46

(xiv)

I stop beside the font where there are pools
of glowing purple daisies. It seems diffusion
from the yellow sun outside is here. A bee
is tumbling in the blooms. This harvest show

could simply be too much
since fruits involve desire,
the need to weigh, describe their valency.
Out of the corner of my eye

I catch a rebus, just an ear
of grain inset oddly by a lady's head.
Her cap is called a butterfly.
Her gown is décolleté, fur outlines

an ample breast, although her upraised hands
are only further details on a little brass.
A massive marrow by her thigh
has tiny marks that show a mouse appreciates

this equinoctial feast. His teeth are accurate
in the display. The sun and moon
could be the minute forces in the space
I clear to rub the brass.

(xv)

The buildings are a group of shacks
where sacking flaps
in holes and not a soul replies
until a moon-faced hand emerges

with some beast. I take the key,
go back to get my tackle as I think
a place like this, though rarely visited,
is much the same whichever way you go

across the fen. This one has a chapel
built to combat spirits in the salt-marsh.
Even I have seen along an inlet
streaks of phosphorescence that were stimulating

in the dark. This very early brass
I've come to rub starts half way down,
his head, in chain, is round, a heart is inching
from his praying grasp. The rest is crudely done

and seems like scales, where I discover
it is hard to fix the paper; so I leave loose
the rolled-up part, and, finding at the lower end
that I go on, strange curves both join the knight

and are detached. I feel about my find
and work the patterns: a serpent is around
a sun and, though there is no person
it appears, a hairy arm

is reaching for a compass
in some twists of sea or wind.
All these are very faint and spread
until I hit the stone. Then as I look about

long since I started on the brass
the disparate effects seem distant; there are
the rough bare walls, the low melancholy wind
that comes in fits and starts, the cold,

the short marked piece of paper.

(xvi)

Not in his ruff a chorister is very near
an organ pedal on the right. I have to brush
the dust away and shine my torch
about the narrow space, the cassocks

getting smaller down the row. It's not easy
to fit in because I'm not inclined to move too much
that isn't mine, remembering the master's touchiness
and knowing that we had to sing without accompaniment

whilst he would creep along
and listen for the boy whose pitch was wrong.
I was discovered, had to sing alone
and in the candlelight apparently looked bloodless.

I always thought I was a pleasant treble, notes
alighting on bright colours high above the stalls.
In rousing from my reverie I find I'm wedged,
still rubbing, glad to see the singing-boy

is ready to go out; indeed he takes a step,
his muffler blowing; and he has a stick, an odd effect,
with which he seems to point his way.
I remember how I left and pelted at the graves.

(xvii)

We count between the flash
and the report, a snapped off crack.
Over the extent of flat land fields of wheat
take on an extra tawniness against

advancing black. The quivers in the sky
could penetrate to our crusader, rubbed
in gold and still attached, except
together, standing in the porch, we shield

the light. We laughed in bringing out the rub
that we were no pet creatures
at his feet. The lion's tail is whipped
beside a spur, the sword demands a massive grip

and scoops for winnowing are bold across his shield
and surcoat. As many roots
of lightning snake and hit the earth, I think,
although it isn't natural, the complicated lines

we've worked in heat before the storm
could be those sudden veins. We turn away:
a blinding burst of white comes at us. Shapes
at that moment have no light and shade.

He seems to twitch as, waiting inside,
we can't help but watch a constant flicker
over his great form, until at last unbroken dark
and hissing rain provide relief.

We remark uncomfortably that we must hang him
in a gloomy place to get the benefit of how he shines.

(xviii)

The choristers are practising at Christmas time.
Sometimes a quiet testy voice arrests
a rising note. These stops interrupt me,
but it is right to take instruction

since fine emphases mean much
to educated ears. The place at which I work
is down the nave. I only half attend
to how I go, the rubbing having nothing in

the way of pieces which extend beyond
the major shape. I prefer a brass with hints
of movement like a hand that slightly moves
to put a fold in place, and thus

this bulk, which has few chinks
to give relief, his psalter even gripped
against his solar plexus, must prevent
much interest. "Commercial rig!" goes through

my head, but then it could be said
it lets me stretch and see the boys through leaves
along the screen. They shift a little
and would surely like a song with running notes.

The master has to mention discipline as I admire
the richness of the scene. Each candle
in its glass is trim along black wood.
"It is an ancient problem, gentlemen:

you dot the 'I's." The man is lean, erect,
and at a well-pruned gesture they all follow him,
there being not a sign of slackness in their stance
because they know they must be straight to breathe

and be composed. Their purple robes are smooth
and moulded in the yellow light. I leave the brass
and give my whole attention to the flowing
melancholy joy of "Jesus Christ the Apple Tree".

(xix)

She had had a hand in rubbing him,
had been excited when she saw him
on the stairs and cried, "The head
    is mine!" And now he moves in dreams,

he roars, his eyes are flaming,
so she says. What silliness! Resist
such fictions! Wax and paper!
Of course we take him down,

at which she stares
and looks reproachful, meaning, I would guess,
the space declares her fear.
The "hangits" then provide us swords.

But that is neither joke nor therapy
to her. She jabs as I begin
to strike an attitude. I could swear
this girl is awkward, not the child

who shouted for protection in the night
and made me understand how firm
he stood and stamped. And now
she says that she would like the skeleton

and gets it out. "That's wild!"
I have to say. "We always have one there";
she smiles and dances round.
She holds it by a toe.

(xx)

I read no further than "Sic transit . . ."
on another brass beside me. I'm otherwise
absorbed. It is cold and quiet
here. Infrequently, I'm conscious of

distorted reedy sounds as someone tries
to mend an organ. There is a story
that the clerk I work went deaf, his hours
having to be spent in copying the homilies

his mistress emphasized must shape the prayers
he had to say for her when she was dead,
the thought of which calls up the moral absolutes
which, underneath a brass, are meant to harrow us.

A wierd vibration does not startle me,
perhaps because the air is numbing.
That his death preceded hers seems good
as I strip off the rub

and know the plate is scarcely altered.
The workman had observed
the neutral gaze, a blank surround,
a rosary, the ordinary garb, and in a corner

added just a sprig of rosemary.

54

(xxi)

Though there is little time, I look back across
this chilly rippled mere. It is said the church
from which I took the rub was built on the assumption
that the nearby estuary would be a staple port.

But new currents brought the silt and disappointment
for the like of the foreshortened man
depicted on the only brass there was.
He does not amount to much; the flowered pouch

across his groin is a very special detail;
the majority seems wooden, square, his head
the too familiar block with stringy locks
and staring eyes. People here are always saying that

this area is shifting still. As a boat is slotting in
the only slip of the horizon I can see from
where I stand, I think about the corner blobs
which represent the missing symbols in the matrix.

Gaps have to have their place no less
than bell-flowers rich in clusters now across
the dune which in particular obscures the view.
How difficult it was to stop the figure riding,

I recall. But part of the product sometimes
seems to be the material not working well.
Also, all the time, in lengthening out
he seemed lost upon the size of paper.

The rub, I feel, is not too unsatisfactory.

(xxii)

I duck in beneath an arch to view
a figure which could be a shining talisman.
He is on a chest, and as I heave to open it
a picture of the waves below comes to me.

The gleaming rollers start far out, where islands
curve into the open sea. The strong current,
wind and sun make white semi-circles round
each piece of land, which as they phase

into the distance neatly seem designed to lead
towards the agitation that the naked eye assumes
in specks. Most turbulence can seem to be in
points that disappear because they are so fine.

Thus the invention of some seamen's myths.
I put back the lid. Extensive mechanisms make
for a smooth fit. The brass compels attention.
He is a splendid thing. His head is bare,

the curling beard is crisp, his hair is shaggy
on his neck, and for such a solid shape
the play about his lips is striking.
The body is in pliant leather.

He is no one, so they tell me. Hence, the relaxation,
I expect. The lock is through an opening
in his chest. There are endless combinations,
exact glinting pins and bars beneath.

56

(xxiii)

An heraldic beast rears as I tip a seat
along a stall. The brass beneath involves
much work where there is hardly any chance
of ease. The boys have kicked away

the lower plate. But there is no reason
why the effort need be unrewarding.
The details on her heart-shaped face
are delicate, the crespine is faceted

with tiny astral shapes, a pearl is hanging
on her neck, and the breast is high
because of the arrangement of a velvet girdle.
In fact it is working well, although the pressure starts

to tell against my side, "the purist" further having
to take pains because he must record the roughness
at the end when it could penetrate the paper. But then
my aches come from the dragon fashioned out

of knots. The resistant fibre must have given
satisfaction as the carver pared
and took his chances. Then moving out I see
the flicking tails, how sharp the darting tongue.

The eyes come at two minute inner rings.
My demi-image has a fringe around her waist.

(xxiv)

I sign the book and read
a number of the other names beside
their comments, "What a lovely place!"
and permutations till my attention

is diverted when a gesture frees
a pen. It swings on its thread
beside a priceless ikon. And
there are other looking-glasses

to attract the vandal. Discovering
the brass does not deserve protection
triggers off a rough reaction,
meaning that I have to try and compensate

with extra pressure. It fails to work.
The frustrating zone extends
as rain is being rapped and scribbled
on a dusty window by a fitful wind;

the glass is long and thin, no bigger
than my paper; it provides
all necessary light. Then I rip off
the mess, and as it floats

I think there is a glimpse of my grimace
upon the brass, a notary. He is humble,
poker-faced and unimpaired. Yet, despite
the tight praying posture

and the prissy well-shaped dress,
the incisive flourish on his ink-horn
and the sharp bones strewn about his feet
take on, far in excess of them,

the need to find a place
for restlessness and force in composition.

58

(xxv)

We manage to unroll the sheet
without a crease. He looks down.
His long wall is void
of decoration. It hurts

because the direct sun floods from
the other side. Best quickly cover him
because he is the centre of the shine.
We mutter when the lime will not respond

to our adhesive, yet somehow
the grey paper holds. Our night out
on the tiles has made us
over sensitive. We neither like

his frown nor that the sun is fixed
in all the polished vessels.
Black be the colour for the upright Judge,
we say, and we digress about

the obscene masons once who drank and had
their women here. But it can't stop there;
as one reclines below, the other
reaches up to rub the narrow face

and oval head, the coif enclosing
any natural line; and then there is the scrawny
over lengthy neck and yards
of cloak. Because I have to stretch

the problem is to give each part
consistency. Easy then to say what more
could we expect from such a censor.
We take a break, exchange some cigarettes

and breathe the middle of the summer day.
The chestnuts seem relaxed old things. Then
my companion wanders off to find a drink
and I am left to think the M.B.S.

are always getting at fun-rubbers. Yet
light charcoal seems the proper base. Let
it be unfinished. Just
keep the face and streaks that tail away.

(xxvi)

The two small early figures sway.
Though they are near
the stone divides them.
It is recorded that their enemies
surprised them at first light.

The man looks down, away,
his chain-mail, it seems, not fitting properly
on a lean awkward body.

She half lifts her hands to pray;
her small visage,
framed in cloth, is sad,
distrait; her pretty mouth
is puckered; now and then a bud
in leaf across her bodice is so sharp
that to the touch it seems above the metal,
although, slanting down, the pattern
disappears. Her gown is loose,
the skirt disturbed
as if a draught has caught it.

A bell begins. The light is growing grey.
The sound wavers coming
through so many cloisters.
But the interruption does not last.

Just after someone touches me to say
it is too late to work successfully, a pause
in the distant chant allows
a note a prolonged echo.
I have been just aware of how
the plainsong has been phrased.
"The effigies are very worn in parts,"
the brother adds as I begin
to gather up my things to leave.

(xxvii)

Sitting on a sleeping statue's coverlet
the children think about my finished rub.
"Say all you can about her," I had said.
"Deploy your adjectives." But they keep quiet.

There are no marks beyond
her edge, and they have said already
that they like the ripple
in her dress. She is visible far

at the building's end
where one of us has sat and waited
with a book. That the rubbing's strength
had altered as the sun had come and gone

and I progressed she'd noticed
as she turned the leaves. My wife is near us
now and sees the faintest inclination
of the head, the circlet's charm,

the long unbraided hair that hides a little
too much of the face. But I tell them haltingly
about the reappearance of the maiden's tired gesture
as she lets her posy hang beside her.

There is nothing we can add.

A CAREFREE RUB

This church would be a long cold place
in winter. Yet round the northern door
there was a rainbow left by village players.
Our children aped some snatches from the Flood.
They made the youngest be the Dove.

Our object was to take a Christmas present
from a frowning brass in chain
and canopied with words about Mortality.
Those intent upon the rub stepped in the rail,
the father being left to nod in musty pews,
"the Dove" to roam and sing
an incoherent tune about a lady and some cherries.
She seemed to stop in sunny places. In surfacing
with half-closed eyes I saw some iridescent touches.
"There's another knight!" she cried.

Indeed there was the saddest little lord
we put upon a scrap of paper. Anyhow, we felt
with blue and silver wax his broken armour,
pinched-in waist and winsome features peeping
for a face. The blur was fine, the aura laughter
as we sneezed in dust beneath a hanging.

I swear that, after we had cut him out, without a trace
of archness she exclaimed, "Let's stick him on the rainbow!"